Distributed to the trade by:
CRESCENT BOOKS
a division of Crown Publishers, Inc.
419 Park Avenue South
New York, N. Y 10016

Charles Laughton

HOLLYWOOD'S
MAGIC
PEOPLE

Charles Laughton

HOLLYWOOD'S MAGIC PEOPLE

by

William Brown

FALCON ENTERPRISES INC. • NEW YORK, NEW YORK • 1970

WITH A COMPLETE LIST OF ALL FILMS, ARTISTS, DIRECTORS, PRODUCERS AND DATE OF PRODUCTION

Page 154

TABLE OF CONTENTS

Piccadilly

Laughton's Gift

Recognition for an actor may come in many forms.

At the upper end of the scale, it comes under glittering lights on the stage of a theatre in Hollywood, before the assembled luminaries of the profession, in the form of an inexpensive but highly prized statuette.

At the folk level, it comes under a single spot on the stampsized dance floor of a night club in the hinterland, as one of God's lost comics earns his

Wolves

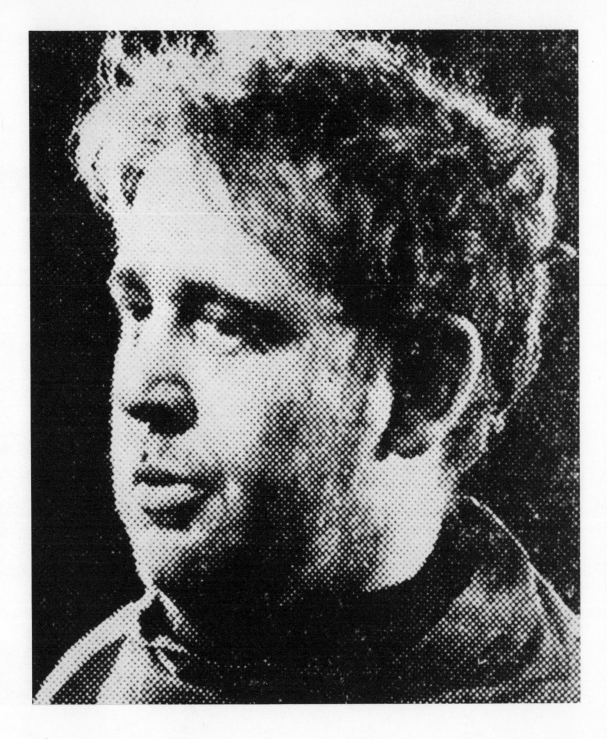

laughs and livelihood mimicking the mannerisms of the stars.

Down near the bottom levels of awareness, it comes in the casual antics of the amateur—making points with his date or the guys in front of the candy store with an imitation of that imitation, or simply with some fleeting bit of pantomime stolen from a performance but lacking even the flimsy structure of a formal take-off.

Charles Laughton earned all these accolades and more.

The role of Henry VIII won him his Oscar, and for years to come a wag just finishing a leg of chicken could win an easy chuckle from his table companions by pretending to launch it over his shoulder to join a phantom pile of bones in the corner.

And who can compute how many impressionists minked their ladies and schooled their get in the

Down River

10

thirties (and, God help us, the forties and fifties, too) by swelling out their bellies, pooching out their lower lips, and bellowing:

"*Mis-tah Christ-yannn!*"

What they were echoing, of course, was Laughton's masterful recreation of Captain Bligh, that dutiful servant of the Crown whose only object was to get a mutinous band of seamen suddenly turned into flower children to lay off the breadfruit and

the local wenches and get the *Bounty* moving again.

Many of Laughton's best-remembered roles were broad, outrageous characterizations, easy enough to ape in Instant Genius.

But it should not be forgotten that there was a time before each of those magic bits of nonsense existed, that every brushstroke of those portraits came into being at the behest of a rare natural man of the theatre.

It was Laughton's special gift to resurrect whole for our time men of another age.

His Henry was a monarch who felt the divine right to the tips of his greasy fingers. He could discard whatever became useless to him with regal disregard—a bone stripped clean of meat, or a tiresome wife. And if the Church object, the Church as well. Refuse disposal was not the business of a king.

As for Bligh, he saw observance of duty and ap-

The Devil and The Deep

12

propriate behavior as outward manifestations of the inner rectitude which was a decent man's most cherished treasure, the fixed star he sailed by, whether in the performance of his daily tasks or adrift alone on the vast Pacific, steered only by the celestial guideposts above and within him.

In such men, Laughton correctly reasoned, very serious springs of action were credibly apt to produce outward behavior that would, and did, seem

Payment Deferred

ludicrous today. The modern individual wouldn't dare to carry on that way, even if he had the rank and position to justify such behavior. Or *thinks* he wouldn't—for modern history is unhappily not devoid of figures of absolute power as laughable as they are terrifying. We are amused by the foibles of tyrants, ancient or contemporary, but we laugh more freely at modern ones only when we're sure they're dead.

A large measure of Laughton's genius was his insight into the workings of the outsized ego. It was the mainstay of his career, but in his first years in Hollywood, it put him at odds with none other than the great De Mille, something of an eccentric power figure himself.

De Mille wanted Laughton for *The Sign of the Cross*, in the part of Nero. De Mille wanted Nero played as the incarnation of wickedness, the de-

The Sign of the Cross

14

stroyer of the Christians, the heartless menace of the ancient world. But Laughton insisted on playing him for laughs.

De Mille was astounded at such a conception. Yet Laughton had devoted considerable study and thought to the part. He had discovered in his researches, for instance, that Nero had fancied himself an actor, and had often compelled his court to watch him perform after locking them in a

If I Had a Million

theatre. It was Laughton's thesis that the excesses of the emperor's rage may have been, at least in part, due to the fact that he'd had to lock them in. In time, the Empire itself had become his captive audience. When the citizenry failed to applaud his increasingly spectacular entertainments, including his ultimate colossal flop, the burning of Rome, it was therefore probably as much hurt anger this vain man felt as sadistic fury.

It took De Mille years to concede Laughton's point, and he never actually admitted publicly that he had, but his remake of *Quo Vadis* featured a Nero played by Peter Ustinov that was a model of merriment and lunatic poetry reading—so apparently De Mille came around at last.

Laughton's conflict with De Mille was not his first disagreement with a legendary monument of his profession, in stubborn defense of an artistic point.

Island of Lost Souls

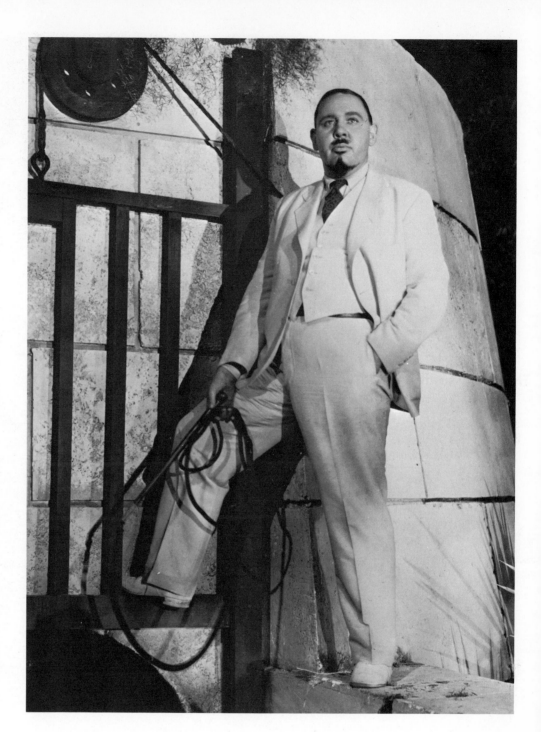

In his very first year as a dramatic student in London, Laughton played the role of Henry Higgins in a workshop production of *Pygmalion*. His approach toward that character, now perhaps best known to us as the irascible but wholly charming professor that Rex Harrison made him in *My Fair Lady*, was closer to what De Mille was later to want in Nero; Laughton played Henry Higgins as a heartless monster.

The Private Life of Henry VIII

George Bernard Shaw, who often attended student productions at the Royal Academy, particularly when his own works were being given, was infuriated, and stormed backstage to straighten out the young actor himself. Laughton's grasp of the dynamics of an ascendant ego may have grown substantially that night. Discussing the incident with Shaw a quarter of a century later, Laughton excused himself by saying he had been "very young."

Young Laughton

Did Laughton first come by his easy familiarity with the odd ways of the exalted during early years at the Laughton country seat?

He did not, for there was none. Charles Laughton made his first entrance in July of 1899 at a railroad hotel owned by his parents in Scarborough, in the North of England.

Robert and Eliza Laughton could only be described as conventional, and it is not a designation

that would have troubled them. Their quarrel with their son was that he was not. His aspirations went straight past the manager's office, out the front door, and down the street to the theatre.

He was unable to make the move physically until he was well into his young manhood. Having successively endured a teenage apprenticeship at Claridge's Hotel in London (spending every spare penny in the galleries of West End), followed by a gas

attack during military service in 1918, and some years thereafter working at the family hotel and consorting evenings with the local amateur theatrical group, Charles at the age of 25 finally persuaded his family to settle a modest allowance on him and let him go to London to attend the Royal Academy of Dramatic Art.

His first task was getting accepted. It is recorded that in preparation for his entrance audition Laugh-

ton rehearsed 19 hours a day, mumbling Shakespeare to himself as he went through the streets. The audition was successful, despite the fact that in his extreme nervousness he sat on his auditioner's hat.

Young Laughton in London became an intense student. He read, he visited the famous galleries and museums and antique fairs; he studied a great quantity of plays, as well as all the appurtenances of stagecraft—the costumes, scenic design, lighting.

22

H.8-187

He was developing the thoroughly professional attitude he would continue to call upon all during his career, for major parts and even for some of the bizarre lesser roles he was destined to have.

Whatever may be said of Laughton by his detractors, it is beyond question that he took his work very seriously, and his attention to the technical skills of acting was devoted. Some might argue that as a result too many of his performances were mechanistic, concerned if anything too largely with external trappings rather than with inner integrity, but Laughton learned his art the conscientious way, feeling that when he could he would build his characters from within, but that when that was not available to him, he would have the resources to create his character the best way he could.

Certainly it is true, with regard to his work in the theatre, that for Laughton it was not merely one

White Woman

facet of an otherwise rich array of interests, it was his life.

While preparations were proceeding for the filming of *The Private Life of Henry VIII* some years later, Laughton spent weeks on his own steeping himself in the lore of the era. He visited and roamed through Hampton Court Palace for days, getting the feel of Tudor architecture and atmosphere generally. He memorized every detail of the famous Holbein por-

trait, which he went to study more than a hundred times, identifying himself with every crease of flesh, every nuance of expression that gave some clue to the inner man who possessed those features. Even today, many who see that same painting are at first struck by its resemblance to someone. The someone is Laughton.

Continuing his researches, Laughton visited London's leading firms of court tailors, knowing that many of them dated from the sixteenth century and reckoning that at least one might still have some authentic record of Henry's costume. He found not one but three such firms; preserved in their files were the very sketches he needed.

So in every way was the Henry that Laughton created as accurate as he could make him; he carefully fashioned a detailed image of the complex ruler, who was, among other things, an accomplished

linguist, a skilled musician who composed two complete Masses—and a wife-butcher, a bone-slinger, and founder of the Church of England.

Such was Laughton's method. Some actors simply interrupt their other pursuits briefly to dip into the background of a role, the externals, concentrating their attention on building their character outward from inner conviction. But Laughton, the man of the theatre, placed great importance on facts and trap-

pings. It may be that through a kind of artistic os-mosis he may actually have learned some inner truth about the kind of man he was to portray in all this rummaging, who knows?

At any rate, this dedicated intensity quite early became apparent to his instructors at the Royal Academy, and they gave him their special attention. Among the more prominent were Alice Gachet, who introduced Laughton to a wealth of French and

British classical drama, and Theodore Komisarjevsky, who guided him through works of Chekhov, Dostoevsky and Gogol.

It was with the assistance of the Russian director that Laughton secured his first paid part, as a drunken servant in Gogol's *The Government Inspector*. It turned out to be a fortunate choice of character, for Laughton suffered acutely from stagefright; he went on stage trembling, and in the grip of a patho-

Ruggles of Red Gap

logical fear that all his clothes would fall from him, leaving him stark naked in front of the audience. It would have been an impressive bit of business, to be sure.

Despite all his fears and jitters, it was nonetheless apparent to all that the young Laughton was possessed of a remarkable voice and presence. His Higgins role in *Pygmalion* came next, and a recitation of the Falstaff scenes from *The Merry Wives of*

Windsor, and Laughton celebrated his first year at the Royal Academy by winning for his work there its highest award, the Bancroft Medal. This unprecedented feat was worthy of mention in the press, and in distant Scarborough an innkeeper began annoying his friends with the clipping from the Times. Eliza Laughton about that time got off a letter to her son inviting him to come home for a visit when he found time.

He did so, but stayed only briefly. He was soon back in London, ransacking that historic city like some open-air museum, from Mayfair to Chinatown. With a growing reputation as a brilliant young actor, he was now in demand socially. His old shyness was fast abating.

Komisarjevsky now called upon Laughton to play the clerk Yepikhodoff in a production of Chekhov's *The Cherry Orchard;* others in the cast included sev-

eral members of the Moscow Art Theatre ensemble. Even though Laughton's part was only twenty-five lines long, it was a well-received production, Komisarjevky's reputation was much enhanced, and with it that of his young student from the Academy.

To capitalize on this success, the Russian director chose as his next project Ferenc Molnar's *Liliom*, with two of the most popular figures of the London stage, Fay Compton and Ivor Novello, as its stars. Laughton

was originally signed for a small part, but while the production was in rehearsal the more substantial role of the thief Ficsur became available, and Laughton gathered his nerve and made a bid for it. After a brief hesitation, Komisarjevsky decided Laughton could do it.

Now began the first and most intense of Laughton's great preparations. It took him into every quarter of London's timeless underworld, and the portrayal that emerged was generally adjudged to be one of uncommon furtiveness, cunning and criminality. The biggest laugh in the play, in fact, came when Laughton as the thief would stare at Liliom with calm and evil innocence and ask, "Do I look like a cheat?"

For the first time, impersonators in the cabarets began doing "Laughton bits." One aspect of the mantle of greatness had begun its descent on the once-shy fat boy with the intense manner.

Les Miserables

Laughton On Stage

Even as Laughton began to taste his first professional success, he was confronted with a professional problem that would bedevil him throughout his career: that actor's nemesis, type-casting.

Already his portrayal of the thief was bringing him offers for parts as criminals, rather than the diversity of roles he both wanted and knew he needed for his artistic development. Though still mainly dependent on the allowance from his family,

In September of that year, Laughton came to America at last, with a triumphant transplant of his London acclaim. The inevitable result, before long, was a rash of offers from Hollywood — all of them, naturally, prompted by the emergence of an exciting new villain, an actor who could ring the various changes of evil to perfection.

If his fame had followed him across the Atlantic, so had Laughton's fate.

he had the patience, confidence and courage to hold out for really challenging offers. In time, one came; he played the part of an elderly, fat general in a play that starred Sybil Thorndike and Basil Gill.

Now, of course, he came to be in some demand as an elderly fat general, but then came an offer which was a genuine departure from anything he had attempted thus far: he was to play an American. At that time, Laughton had never so much as spoken

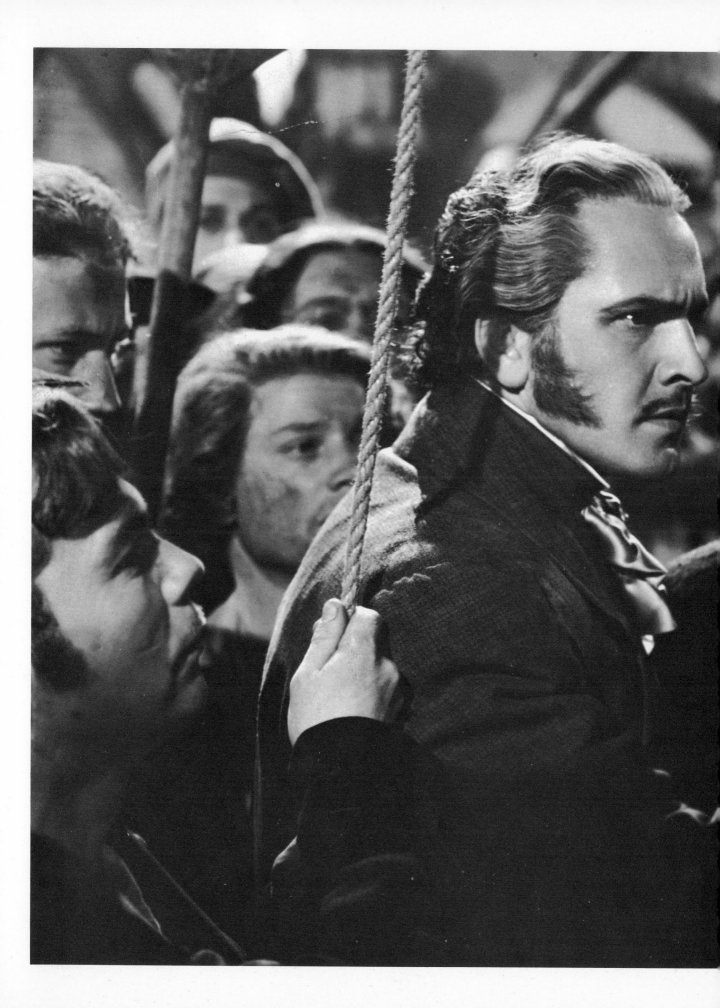

to one.

But he knew what to do; he went to a music shop and asked for a supply of jazz records, and asked also if there were any recordings available of American speech. Yes, he was told, there was one — of their President Wilson.

So it was that shortly thereafter the reedy voice of Woodrow Wilson was heard on the London stage, emanating from the bulk of a rotund young actor

in a play called *The Happy Husband.*

Laughton was something of a sensation, and the word spread across the Atlantic. Now there were offers from New York for him to play American parts (probably including at least one to play Wilson).

Laughton's next major stage vehicle was *Mr. Prohack,* by the English novelist Arnold Bennett, another pillar of British letters who found Laughton's interpretation of his character upsetting. As all London learned when the play opened, the reason Mr. Bennett found Laughton's approach so baffling was that the actor was creating a perfect and hilarious caricature of the author. When Bennett discovered this, too — from the reviews next morning — he was, of course, furious, but calmed down considerably when this, too, became a notable Laughton hit.

It was while working in *Mr. Prohack* that Laughton met Elsa Lanchester, who had a small role in the

Mutiny on the Bounty

play although she had already established a reputation as a comedienne and dancer. Within two years, they would marry.

Elsa was the protege of H. G. Wells, who had written three short plays for her. In 1928, the year after meeting Charles, she went to the studios at Denham to film them. Charles went with her and, more or less for fun, took bit parts in them. He played a rajah in the story called *Daydreams* and a

police constable in the one called *Bluebottles;* both of these films were silent, but the third was an early talkie *On The Spot.* In it, Laughton was able to combine two of his most successful characters by playing a criminal who was an American — of Italian descent.

Wallace invited Laughton to his richly appointed home in order to present the idea to him. He told Laughton the work would be great fun to do; there would be adultery, gunfights, funerals, a kidnapping, plenty of corpses, and a Chinese mistress for Laughton. Laughton is said to have asked only that the gangster's house have purple carpeting and a golden organ for him to play Italian opera on. The two became great friends at once, and remained so — until Wallace wanted him for a second play.

Even while appearing in *On the Spot,* Laughton was energetic enough to appear in yet another film,

Down River, of no particular distinction.

In 1931, the Laughtons had found a pleasant cottage in Surrey and were able to interrupt their careers long enough for a real honeymoon. When they emerged from their retreat and returned to London, it was to take an important step toward worldwide fame; they accepted roles in an adaptation of a C.S. Forester novel called *Payment Deferred.*

In the play, Charles was a murderer; Elsa, his twelve-year-old daughter. Laughton threw himself into the part with his usual gusto, and was soon terrifying audiences with a skillful portrayal of ultra-realistic malevolence. The reviews were so highly complimentary they reached the attention of a leading American producer, Gilbert Miller, who cabled the Laughtons inviting them to recreate their roles on Broadway, at the start of the 1931 season.

In September of that year, Laughton came to America at last, with a triumphant transplant of his London acclaim. The inevitable result, before long, was a rash of offers from Hollywood — all of them, naturally, prompted by the emergence of an exciting new villain, an actor who could ring the various changes of evil to perfection.

If his fame had followed him across the Atlantic, so had Laughton's fate.

Laughton and Hollywood

Dissatisfied with the terms of all the film contract offers, none of which gave him the least say in what roles he would play, Laughton left America with Elsa at the end of the play's run.

Their ship had barely cleared land when a last wireless message arrived from Jesse Lasky of Paramount, substantially agreeing to what Laughton wanted, requiring only that he make two films a year for Paramount in the next three years. The first

would be *The Devil and the Deep*, with Tallulah Bankhead and Gary Cooper, and a script by an old London friend of Laughton's.

Laughton had no choice but to ponder the offer as the ship sailed on for England. Two days after he landed, Laughton decided to accept the offer, repacked hurriedly, and was soon at sea again, heading westward. He was about to begin the greatest adventure of his life, greater even than

leaving Scarborough.

But his arrival in California was far less dramatic than his departure from England. The story is all too familiar from the accounts of other famous personages lured to the film capital and then seemingly forgotten. No one, it appeared, knew who the Laughtons were, precisely, nor why they were there. Paramount was nowhere near ready to make the film. The studio's checks began arriving regularly at

46

the Laughton's hotel — the legendary Garden of Allah — but no message about starting work.

In time, publicity people began to visit them to take stills, providing the bewildered couple with some diversion. Meanwhile, the Laughtons explored the community, the homes of their colleagues and the studios themselves. Typically, Laughton become engrossed in the technical paraphernalia of filmmaking, and began an intensive study of such things

as the differences between movie and stage lighting, make-up, camera angles, sound recording. His work in the British films, he soon realized, had been only a perfunctory introduction to the intricacies of this new craft. The prodigious resources of the Hollywood studios made the British ones seem almost primitive by comparison.

Still the waiting continued; Paramount was still engaged in its preparations for the film that Laugh-ton had come to make, having accepted the contract which seemed his best chance to avoid the "evil" stereotype. Then Laughton was informed that in the meantime another studio, Universal, had asked if it might borrow his services for a film by the English writer, J. B. Priestly.

This much sounded perfectly agreeable to Laugh-ton. Then came further details. The script was called *The Old Dark House*. Laughton's part would be

R.B.446.

48

small; the star would be another promising young visitor from England, Boris Karloff, who would play a demented servant. The director was someone Elsa knew; he had been her stage manager in an English revue called *Riverside Nights*: James Whale. (It was the combination of Whale directing Karloff that produced the horror classic, *Frankenstein*. Elsa was later to make a sequel with them, *The Bride of Frankenstein*.) Dismayed at first, Laughton brightened some-

R.B.81A

what when he learned that he would play a rather jolly businessman. At any rate, it was better than waiting.

Paramount was immensely pleased by what they undoubtedly considered Laughton's extended screen test, produced for them as well as the public by Universal. Laughton's close study of the special techniques of the medium had been most productive; he had learned the new art of acting for the camera to virtual perfection.

And so finally Paramount began production of *The Devil and the Deep*, with Laughton as a submarine commander who is the jealous husband of Miss Bankhead, and who decides to ram his sub into an ocean liner in order to kill his wife, her lover, Gary Cooper, and himself.

The story, of course, sounds absolutely preposterous today, but early films were dependent for their

50

success in no small measure on their ability to show scenes of action that could never be so crediby depicted in a theatre, and such spectacles as the ramming of the liner were a standard crowd-pulling element of the movies' bag of tricks. In fact, such spectacles are occasionally the chief virtue of some films made even today.

At any rate, the story notwithstanding, the cast's work made the picture an affecting film, especially

I, Claudius

Laughton's high moment, a remarkably realistic underwater death scene which took twenty-three straight hours to shoot.

And so, presently, came the call from Mr. De Mille about Nero.

The wrangling between Laughton and De Mille was no mere meaningless clash of temperments; it was a crucial point in Laughton's career, and he was quite literally fighting for his artistic life in films.

If he had acceded without question to De Mille's much shallower conception of the part of Nero, it would not only have been a great disservice to his own ability to build a complicated character, it would have meant as well his surrender at the outset to a succession of mediocre roles foisted upon him by even less imaginative men. On the other hand, if Laughton succeeded in maintaining his interpretation despite De Mille's view, he would have won

The Beachcomber

for himself a considerable measure of artistic integrity and freedom in future roles.

If Laughton had not prevailed at that crucial moment in the early 1930s, we would never have seen the incredible performances he won the right to give in the years after his unpredictable romp as Nero.

It must be admitted that even if Laughton had meekly accepted direction, *The Sign of the Cross*, like all of De Mille's films, was destined to be an

international box office smash. Nevertheless, Laughton had won his license to act, and while Paramount digested the implications of this unexpected development, it decided to lend his services to still another Titan of that era, Metro-Goldwyn-Mayer's brilliant Irving Thalberg.

It was sometimes an aspect of Mr. Thalberg's genius to see the obvious when everyone else had overlooked it. It is in the classic tradition of Holly-wood legend that Irving Thalberg now wanted Laughton to make for M-G-M the film version of the play that had prompted Paramount to sign him in the first place, *Payment Deferred*.

It is even more classic that the part of the murderer's twelve-year-old daughter was given not to Elsa Lanchester but to Maureen O'Sullivan.

And it is most classic of all that the picture closed in New York after two days.

Meanwhile, Paramount, having ruminated on what to do with the genuine actor they had placed under contract, assigned Laughton to his second picture for them: *The Island of Lost Souls*. The cast would also include Richard Arlen and Bela Lugosi, plus a veritable menagerie. Laughton would play an evil scientist who had discovered a process for changing men into beasts. The island of the title would be Catalina, toward which Paramount soon launched a

vile-smelling craft laden with animals, whips and extras.

After perhaps a small sigh, Laughton summoned his conscientious professionalism and began work on his make-up. At about this time, suffering a minor malady of the eye, he visited an oculist. He was fascinted by the man's appearance, especially the tiny, wicked-looking beard he wore. Even as he read the doctor's eye chart, he was making mental notes

concerning his features. It was this harmless eye doctor Laughton recreated for his mad scientist in the film.

One noteworthy outcome of this doubtful venture — actually, not a bad specimen of the genre, with a script based on a story by H. G. Wells — was that it was officially banned in England as being ''against the laws of nature.''

(''So is Mickey Mouse,'' Elsa snorted for the press

Sidewalks of London

56

from England, where she'd returned to do some work.)

In this same period, an opportunity Laughton found irresistable was working with the great master of comedy, Ernst Lubitsch, who offered Laughton a small part in a picture he was making called *If I Had a Million*. The film would consist of eight separate episodes, featuring such stars as Gary Cooper, George Raft, Richard Bennett (the father of

Constance and Joan), Jack Oakie and W. C. Fields.

Laughton enjoyed his role immensely, as well as the director and the pleasant company. He played a mousy clerk who is selected by chance to receive a gift of a million dollars, and thereupon runs up an interminable flight of stairs in order to give the president of the firm a glorious raspberry. (It was so effective that Lubitsch had to shoot a toned-down version for England.)

Having come to Hollywood intending to fulfill his contract obligation to make two films, Laughton in his first full year in America had now made six pictures, in his voracious, perhaps injudicious, appetite to be about his craft. If he had lent his talent to some enterprises that were questionable, there was yet his Nero.

But Elsa was in England, and something of Laughton's English identity and his creative aspira-

CHARLES LAUGHTON

JAMAICA INN

with MAUREEN O'HARA · LESLIE BANKS · EMLYN WILLIAMS · ROBERT NEWTON
FROM THE NOVEL BY DAPHNE DU MAURIER · A POMMER-LAUGHTON "MAYFLOWER" PRODUCTION
Directed by ALFRED HITCHCOCK · A Paramount Release · Produced by ERICH POMMER

58

tions, too. It was with some trepidation about the sort of welcome he would receive in his homeland after his Western adventure that Laughton set sail for his sources.

Awaiting him there was the great triumph of his career, the masterpiece role his skill would approach again, but never surpass: Henry.

CHARLES LAUGHTON

JAMAICA INN

with MAUREEN O'HARA · LESLIE BANKS · EMLYN WILLIAMS · ROBERT NEWTON
FROM THE NOVEL BY DAPHNE DU MAURIER · A POMMER-LAUGHTON "MAYFLOWER" PRODUCTION
Directed by ALFRED HITCHCOCK · A Paramount Release · Produced by ERICH POMMER

Laughton's Masterpiece

Making another film was probably the furthest thing from Laughton's mind as he returned to England in 1932.

He went immediately to Surrey, to relax. He was looking forward toward getting back on the stage, perhaps trying his luck with the Old Vic, nourishing his craft through exposure to the great classics of theatrical literature. It would not only clear his head of all the goblins he'd been surrounded by in Holly-

1812 - 168

MF3/197

62

wood, it would demonstrate that he was fully cap-
able of handling the depths of the great stage roles.

Still, he had been enormously impressed by the
massive technical skill brought to bear by the Hollywood people, even in producing the lowliest horror
film. The professionals who were gathering in California from all over the world were undeniably creating the center of the new industry; it would be
ten years at least before the English studios could

1812-5
MF3/87

turn out anything to challenge the output of Hollywood's "mills" — as he called them in an interview on his arrival.

This last opinion, though at least partly a shrewd quote calculated to make good copy for the English papers, was probably a fair reflection of his judgment at the time: Hollywood for films, and the money; London for the stage.

But Laughton's agent urged him to talk to Alexander Korda, then a relatively little known film maker, who wanted to star the Laughtons in a film called A Gust of Wind. Though probably tempted for personal reasons by the chance to do something with Elsa, it was Shakespeare he was after. He said he was not interested.

In Paris for a weekend, Laughton ran into Korda again. At dinner, Korda now had a new suggestion: making a film about one of the great English kings,

The Hunchback of Notre Dame

Henry VIII. At last, Shakespeare! But no, as it developed, Korda had a modern script, done by a Hungarian writer, Lajos Biro.

Laughton listened on through dinner. As Korda explained it, the story would offer a psychological explanation of the motivation for Henry's behavior. The part would have real depth and roundness, after all.

But, Korda warned, it could not be a lavish pro-

duction; funds were not available for that. The actors themselves would have to put up some of the money, and costs would have to be kept to a minimum. The story and the performances would have to carry the day, not the sets and costumes.

As might be expected, the plan challenged Laughton's ego, as it was probably meant to. It would be a chance to out-Shakespeare Shakespeare by creating his own Henry, a Henry no classical actor had ever had the chance to play. Seen in this light, Korda's proposal had nothing to do with merely "making another film" — it was a venture into a new realm.

And so Laughton decided to put up the money he had made in Hollywood and have a go at it.

Preparations for the film began soon afterward, and went on for many weeks, including Laughton's own researches at Hampton Court Palace and else-

66

where. But when shooting started, production went quickly and was completed in just five weeks; the film was made for approximately $50,000.

The making of *Henry* was a pioneering endeavor in many ways, not least in that its principal star was also involved in the financing of the film. As a result, Laughton now devoted his intensity not only to the creation of his part, but to as many other aspects of the production as time and Korda permitted.

Having worked with the great De Mille, for instance, Laughton was able to offer suggestions for
the setting of the great banquet scene. For such
lavish effects, he told Korda, it would be a great
mistake to skimp and think only of the budget. In
consequence, for the banquet scene enough van-
loads of food were laid on to feed every unemployed
actor in London (as it well may have).

Laughton had numerous suggestions for the

script, too — how the character of Henry might
better be established by a change in dialogue here,
or perhaps the addition of a scene there, to point
up some facet of his nature.

Elsa made a fine Anne of Cleves; she played a
hilarious wedding-night scene with Charles that
found her beating him at cards and finally talking
him into getting a divorce rather than having her
beheaded. The film also featured outstanding per-

HO-246

They Knew What
They Wanted

formances by Robert Donat, Binnie Barnes, Merle Oberon and Wendy Barrie — but it was Laughton's film, of course — no contest. He had taken full advantage of an actor's golden dream, the opportunity to dominate a production totally, as would not be done again until Orson Welles. The result was not the shambles such a situation might have produced, but a tasteful and magnificent tour de force. Alexander Korda was eventually knighted for his

contributions to the British film industry, and thus to the Exchequer; Laughton never was. But let history note that this film, permeated as it was with Charles Laughton's genius, was the first foreign-made film to win the Best Picture of the Year Award of the American Academy of Motion Picture Arts and Sciences.

It would, as Laughton correctly foresaw, be another ten years before the era of J. Arthur Rank and quantities of English films comparable to the output of Hollywood's mills, but artistic recognition for the product of a British studio dates from *The Private Life of Henry VIII,* starring Charles Laughton.

As for Charles, although he got no title, he was given a little statuette of his own for his Best Performance as Henry. It was the only Oscar he ever won.

Laughton's Prime

Even before the trade premiere of *Henry*, Laughton sailed for America to continue fulfilling his commitment to Paramount.

The studio had prepared a richly rewarding part for him to follow the artistic exertions of the past few months; he would play a Cockney named Horace Prin who was the ruthless ruler of an African river empire. The film, based on a Broadway turkey some Eastern employee had acquired and which therefore

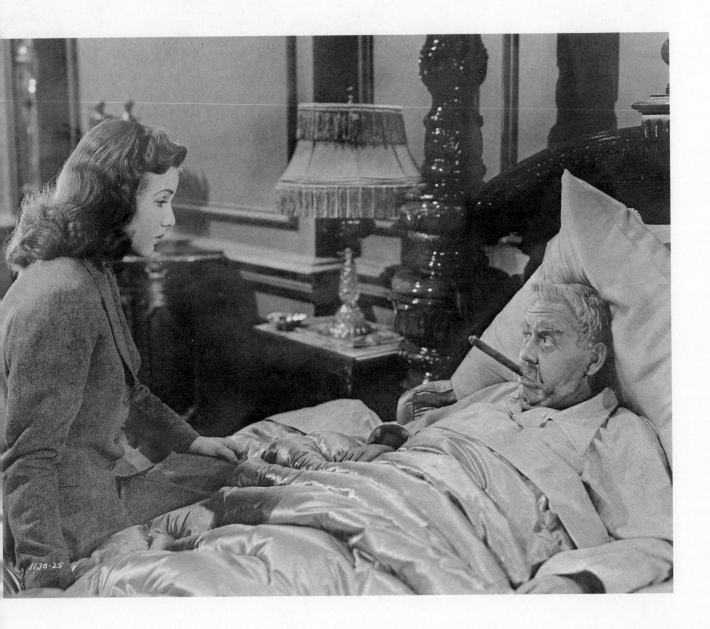

had to be made, would be called *White Woman.* The other stars would be Carole Lombard, Kent Taylor, Charles Bickford, Percy Kilbride and Ethel Griffies. Laughton made it without a fuss, then took the money and the boat. He had promises to keep.

The official premiere of *Henry,* in Paris, was the signal for a whole new flood of film offers — including, one may be sure, many to play fat kings who were monsters.

Laughton chose instead to join a stock company for the equivalent of $100 a week — playing Shakespeare. The group was the Sadler's Wells Company, the Old Vic. Others in the company for the 1933-34 season included Mrs. Laughton and Flora Robson; among the student actors given minor parts that year were Marius Goring and James Mason. The repertory included *The Cherry Orchard, The Importance of Being Earnest,* and Shakespeare's

The Tuttles of Tahiti

Henry VIII, Measure for Measure, The Tempest, and *Macbeth.*

The season has been called Laughton's "offering on the altar of drama."

According to the critics of the day, the offering consisted of overripe ham.

From the experience, Laughton developed new resources in the instrument of his voice. But for his dream of demonstrating his command of Shakes-

peare, the season was a disaster.

Night after night, Laughton wrestled with the Bard, and both lost. Having developed a technique ideally suited to the camera, Laughton now felt he must stop underplaying and let himself out — and so overacted abominably. He attempted to leaven his portraits of the classic figures with the delightful comic touches that had so nicely set off his film portrayals, and they fell flat. So he resorted to stepped-up emotion and shouting. His fellow actors and the audiences were appalled.

In fairness to Laughton, it must be pointed out that many another fine actor has broken his lance against the supreme test of Shakespeare — Sir Alec Guinness as Hamlet among recent examples. The experience is always at once humbling and enlarging.

After eight months of this torture, the season ended and it was time for Laughton to return to

Tales of Manhattan

Hollywood and make the last film under his contra[ct] to Paramount.

First, however, Laughton accepted an offer fro[m] Thalberg: he could have the role of Mr. Barrett i[n] *The Barretts of Wimpole Street* — if he lost fift[y] pounds.

The role of the tyrannical father of Elizabet[h] Barrett, the frail poetess who falls in love wit[h] Robert Browning, was an excellent one, Laughto[n]

knew. Frederic March and Norma Shearer would have the parts of the lovers, and Thalberg was prepared to give the film the care and attention it deserved. So Laughton embarked on a diet, starving himself as he watched Norma Shearer gorging herself (or so it seemed in his hunger), and made the weight and the part.

It was a villain's role, and for the most part Laughton played it heavy, as Thalberg wanted. Yet,

there were certain comic overtones at which audiences insisted upon laughing. Laughton had turned in, it was generally conceded, a superb performance. Thalberg was delighted, and offered to place Laughton under personal contract when his obligations to Paramount ended. His first picture would be *Marie Antoinette*, with Norma Shearer in the title role and Laughton as Louis XVI. As it turned out, this project had to be shelved when Norma Shearer,

Mrs. Thalberg, became pregnant.

Laughton at this time had become ill enough to require surgery. During his convalescence, a frequent cheering visitor was the director Josef von Sternberg, who was in the process of turning Marlene Dietrich into an institution.

On the mend, Laughton reported to Paramount, to make *Ruggles of Red Gap*, directed by Leo Mc Carey, in which Laughton plays an English butler

80

won by a rancher in a poker game and transported to the American West of the 1900s as the proprietor of a frontier saloon. With a cast including Mary Boland, ZaSu Pitts, and Roland Young, Laughton gave a fine comic performance climaxed by a moving rendition of Lincoln's Gettysburg Address.

Close upon this success followed another; Laughton played the part of the heartless policeman Javert in *Les Miserables*, directed for United Artists by Richard Boleslawski and starring Frederic March as Jean Valjean. Laughton, in a striking uniform he helped create himself, was a relentless image of justice, pursuing Valjean without pause, even through the sewers of Paris. One of the film's moments of high drama is Laughton's courtroom speech, in which he explains his devotion to the law, recalling that his mother was a gypsy, his father died on the gallows, and he himself was born in a prison.

In that same year, 1935, Laughton signed the contract with Thalberg and began work on his first picture under the agreement.

Thalberg, prompted by the success of a popular history of the event, was producing a film called *Mutiny on the Bounty.* It was to be one of the most ambitious screen undertakings of its day. Thalberg was determined that the film should be accurate and authentic in every detail.

To produce background photography for the action, Thalberg and director Frank Lloyd sent a crew of fifty technicians and bit players all the way to Tahiti; the stars went only as far as Catalina, the island of lost souls.

Researchers crossed the Pacific in an effort to locate, if they could, the original logbook of the Bounty; ten months later they found it in Syndey, Australia.

The scholarly digging set in motion by the film unearthed considerable new information about the events surrounding the mutiny and the subsequent lives of the mutineers, and added in some measure to anthropological knowledge. Partly as a result of the interest stimulated by the film, scientists devoted closer attention to the modern inhabitants of Pitcairn Island, descended from the ship's crew and their Polynesian brides, and discovered a number of fas-

Forever and a Day

cinating remnants of the English culture of the late 1700s preserved in isolation from the ongoing stream of world events.

Few motion pictures in the history of the medium can be said to have generated so much useful activity in their wake. That, and the remarkable performances of the entire cast — among them Clark Gable as Fletcher Christian, Franchot Tone, Dudley Digges and Donald Crisp — mark this picture as one of the

major landmarks of the industry's development.

As brilliantly as all the other members of a fine and well-integrated cast played, it is beyond question Charles Laughton's vivid interpretation of Captain Bligh which lives most unforgettably in the mind's eye of all who saw it.

The picture was remade in 1962, for some unfathomable reason. Although Marlon Brando added distinctive and revealing insights into the character of Fletcher Christian, with subtleties that were not available to Gable (who didn't need and wouldn't have wanted them, in any case), Captain Bligh as played by that otherwise excellent actor Trevor Howard seems reduced almost to being a minor annoyance to the crew, in contrast to Laughton's Bligh — who brooded over every moment of the drama, an engulfing presence, a somber force of icy retribution that was Javert raised to the hun-

This Land is Mine

dredth power.

From the beginning, Laughton was aware that Captain Bligh was destined to be one of the chief roles of his career, and he determined to bring to the part the full resources of his imagination, his intelligence, and his training.

In keeping with the aura of authenticity which attached itself to the production, Laughton, finding finding himself in London as preparations went

ahead, decided to visit once again the venerable tailors of Bond Street.

In years to come, it would give him much amusement to tell the story of how he had asked the first clerk he saw to provide him with a duplicate of the naval uniform made by the firm for one Captain Bligh. Deadpan, the clerk asked only, "What year?" and was back with the sketches and measurements in a matter of moments.

Inwardly, Laughton addressed himself no less assiduously to piecing together the motivation of a man who could do the stern, uncompromising things which history sets forth Bligh actually did. It required of Laughton a very fine concentration to build to just the right pitch of self-righteous tyrannical command without falling over into the ludicrous. Laughton maintained his balance perfectly, neither pressing too hard nor holding his force in check for fear

The Man from Down Under

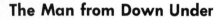

92

of overdoing it, providing the exact amount of intensity held at the limit of tolerance.

In many ways, this was the finest and most workmanlike job of acting Laughton ever did, in a number of respects an advance beyond even his strutting Henry; it won him a second nomination for the Academy Award that year. Coincidentally, however, it was the same year in which Victor McLaglen came up with the one great performance of his life,

Gyppo in *The Informer,* and the Oscar went instead to him.

While the enormous success of *Bounty* was still fresh, Laughton now heard again from Korda. He was planning a production based on the Robert Graves novel, *I Claudius,* with von Sternberg directing. Laughton was to have the great fun of creating yet another despotic Roman emperor. Meanwhile, the prospects for the future in Hollywood were brighter than ever; Laughton and Thalberg had begun making plans for Laughton to become a producer himself, exercising far greater control over his films.

He sailed again for England in high spirits, and was on the train from Geneva to Rome for Korda's film when he received word from Hollywood that, at the age of thirty-seven, Irving Thalberg was dead.

What films might have followed *Mutiny on the*

94

Bounty from Thalberg and Laughton we can only wonder and guess. Laughton's destiny now lay with Korda.

Claudius did not go well. It was rumored that Korda was dissatisfied with the way von Sternberg was directing the script. Then, with only two reels completed, Korda's wife, Merle Oberon, who had the female lead, was injured in an auto accident. And so the entire project was scrapped.

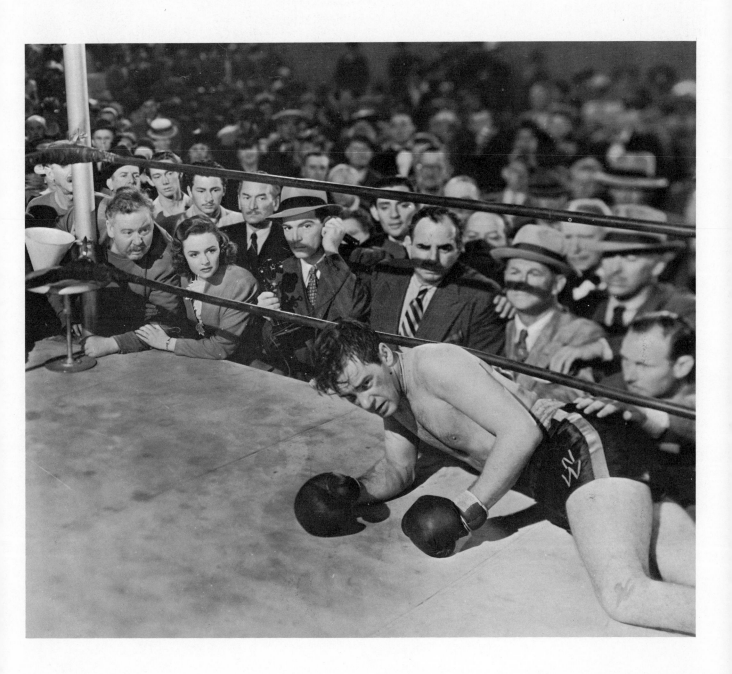

It had not been an auspicious year for Korda projects; his earlier plan to star Laughton and Oberon in *Cyrano* had fallen through when he failed to find a satisfactory script.

With Thalberg gone and Korda momentarily becalmed, Charles Laughton, at the peak of his powers and world acclaim, still in his thirties, found himself without a contract, without a role to play or even prepare for.

In this interval occurred a completely unpredictable diversion: Maurice Chevalier, the French entertainer, approached Laughton with the cheerfully irrational suggestion that he consent to appear in a midnight benefit performance of Moliere with the Comedie Francaise. He would be the first English actor to appear with the theatre's company in its three-hundred-year history. He would have five days in which to prepare his part, in French.

Naturally, Laughton agreed — and went on to receive notices of astonished praise for a courageous and flawless performance (which occurred sometime after two in the morning).

In time, Alexander Korda was back in action, offering Laughton a new vehicle which would be a fitting challenge for his abilities: *Rembrandt*.

Once more back in harness, Laughton plunged into another campaign of massive research and

preparation. For his benefit, the director of Amsterdam's leading museum rounded up a collection of almost every work by the painter in Europe. Laughton spent hours before them, particularly the self-portraits. He read every book he could find on the artist, searched out and pored over his correspondence. He roamed through Holland, absorbing the sight and feel of the country. He devoted day after day to experiments with his appearance and make-up; with features that had long since become malleable to his wishes, he succeeded in making one of his eyes seem smaller than the other, as Rembrandt's had. The make-up for the role would be especially difficult; the artist would have to age from 35 to 60.

The film, which also starred Elsa Lanchester and Gertrude Lawrence as the women in the painter's life, had an especially sensitive and poetic script by Carl Zuckmayer. The part required of Laughton a far

98

more delicate characterization than any he had ever
played. The sometimes obtrusive cleverness, the
bluster, and the pre-occupation with externals which,
for some, marred many of his best-remembered creations were muted and softened in his gentle, carefully constructed insight into a man of artistic genius
rather than of sweeping action. For many who did
not much care for anything else Laughton ever did,
his *Rembrandt* occupies a special niche of honor in

his career.

Perhaps because of the troubled condition of world affairs in that time, as it became steadily more apparent that war was inevitable, perhaps because so sensitive a film was in advance of public taste, *Rembrandt* never achieved the popular recognition of Laughton's great triumphs, and his fine performance has been virtually forgotten by most except his staunchest fans.

Free again of commitments and in a mood to indulge his whims, Laughton followed his portrayal of *Rembrandt* by playing the role of Captain Hook in a London holiday production of *Peter Pan,* with Elsa, of course, as Peter. But Sir James Barrie, then still living, insisted on close supervision of the production, for fear Laughton would terrify the children. He cramped Laughton's style and spoiled the experience completely.

It was a critical time for Laughton. In a surprisingly brief time, he had chalked up a series of brilliant successes and placed himself high in his profession. In the early years, in his restless eagerness to try everything, and partly from financial need, he had sometimes expended his talents on more than a few undeserving enterprises. Though there was no calling them back now, Laughton felt with increasing conviction that if he were to go on any more flyers he

should at the very least maintain the maximum power of choice as to what they would be and how they would be done.

Thus, he marked the end of this phase of his career in 1937 by joining with Erich Pommer, the former production head at Germany's leading studio, UFA — and the man who had made *The Cabinet of Dr. Caligari* there in 1919 — to form a new film company called Mayflower Productions.

Pommer and Laughton launched their Mayflower with three properties: a Somerset Maugham story called *Vessel of Wrath,* a Clemence Dane screenplay called *St. Martin's Lane,* and a screen adaptation of Daphne du Maurier's novel *Jamaica Inn.*

Vessel of Wrath (released in America as *The Beachcomber*) offered Laughton a fine comedy role as a free-drinking remittance man in the South Seas named Ginger Ted; Elsa played the missionary,

The Canterville Ghost

Martha Jones, who reforms and eventually marries him. The cast had a fine time making the picture in the south of France, and Laughton was at his high comic best, but the film was not overwhelmingly profitable.

St. Martin's Lane (released in America as *The Sidewalks of London*) was notable chiefly for an early appearance of Vivien Leigh as a poor girl whom Laughton works into his streetsinger act and

guides on to stardom; others in the cast were Rex Harrison, Tyrone Guthrie, the harmonica virtuoso Larry Adler, and any number of remarkable English street entertainers. The film's strong English flavor was too exotic for it to be successful in America; it was released in the United States only after Vivien Leigh's performance as Scarlett O'Hara in *Gone With the Wind*.

Mayflower had now made two stabs at commer-cial success and missed; it needed a solid hit to stay above water. *Jamaica Inn* would have to do. Having secured J. B. Priestly to write the dialogue, Pommer and Laughton hired Alfred Hitchcock to direct, and rounded up a large and competent cast that in-cluded Maureen O'Hara, Emlyn Williams and Robert Newton; Laughton himself would play the leader of a band of land pirates who plagued the Cornish coast in the eighteenth century.

106

The combination of talents that was to have been ideal soon ran into snags over personality differences. Hitchcock in his early films had already developed his very distinctive approach, deeply grounded in a personal use of the medium's techniques, strongly dependent on a pace of action that was incompatible with Laughton's development of his character. Each was right on his own, together they were totally at odds. Moreover, communication be-

tween Hitchcock and Pommer was especially poor.

Laughton had planned next to star in *The Admirable Crichton* if Mayflower remained afloat, but after *Jamaica Inn*'s poor box office showing he was forced to concede that his attempted voyage to independence was premature.

After an absence of four years, Laughton set sail again for Hollywood, deferring his plans until another day.

The Suspect

HIS WAS A STRANGE **SECRET!**

HERS WAS A STRANGE **LOVE!**

Charles **LAUGHTON**
Ella **RAINES**
in

Suspect

The

with DEAN HARENS

STANLEY C. RIDGES · HENRY DANIELL

ROSALIND IVAN

Laughton in Search of Laughton

He had accepted the role of Quasimodo in *The Hunchback of Notre Dame*, a re-make of the silent classic. He would be in historical competition with one of the more remarkable creations of the legendary Lon Chaney.

Laughton now placed himself in the hands of RKO's make-up department, which outdid itself in hiding Laughton's face in a cascade of rubber ugliness that entirely obliterated one of his eyes, repro-

Captain Kidd

ducing it further down on his cheek. He was all but unrecognizable in the part, even to himself at the premiere, and it is a tribute to his pure physical histrionic ability that, stripped of the power of his expressive features, he was able to convey with the movements of his misshapen body the tremendous pathos of the character. It was a formidable acting achievement, but the part troubled and disgusted him.

RKO's next offer to Laughton was to dust off his Italian accent, last used for the gangster in Edgar Wallace's play, for *They Knew What They Wanted*, co-starring Carole Lombard. The producer was Pommer, who after fleeing Germany under Hitler had come to Hollywood when Mayflower sank; the director was Broadway's Garson Kanin. As an uneducated man who cripples himself in his exuberance at taking a mail-order bride, Laughton was disappointing.

Because of Him

112

At the studio's behest, Laughton agreed to make his first public appearance tour on behalf of the picture. For his appearances, he determined to avoid star-talk and chit-chat, and worked up a series of recitations composed of Shakespeare, the Bible, some of the more poetic lines from *Rembrandt,* and similar respectable material. To his surprise, the tour was received far better than the picture.

In his next film, Laughton played the part of a

lovable, largely bed-ridden elderly matchmaker in a comedy starring Robert Cummings and Deanna Durbin called *It Started with Eve*.

The world, America included, was now in the grip of war. Film output in America consisted more and more of patriotic movies and frothy comedies; few films had either ambitious budgets or artistic pretensions. The great roles were no longer forthcoming for Laughton. His homeland was fighting for its

existence. He had offered the British government his services in any capacity it chose, but had been told to continue with what he was doing. What he was doing was, for the most part, terrible.

In 1942 he clowned through a Beachcomberish role in *The Tuttles of Tahiti,* made an appearance as a symphony conductor whose rented tailcoat splits at the seams when he finally makes it to Carnegie Hall in *Tales of Manhattan,* was miscast as an ad-

114

miral in a Robert Taylor flag-waver called *Stand By for Action*, played a butler in a 79-star film called *Forever and a Day*, was a French schoolteacher standing up to the Nazis in *This Land is Mine*, and played an Australian bar-owner in *The Man from Down Under*.

Having appeared in this series of minor roles dur-the early forties, Laughton created something of his old sparkle as *The Canterville Ghost*, directed by

The Big Clock

Jules Dassin prior to his Greek-earthiness period, and with little Margaret O'Brien before she got completely out of hand. Others who abetted Laughton's delightful whimsy were Robert Young, Peter Lawford, William Gargan, Reginald Owen, Rags Ragland, and Una O'Connor.

Aside from this relief from the series of trivial parts he was getting, Laughton's only other escape hatch was the activity he had chosen as his personal war effort: visiting veterans' hospitals and reading to the wounded servicemen.

Most of his audiences for these readings were young men who were totally unfamiliar with most of the classic and even the popular literature he presented. To reach them and prepare them for these works, Laughton would often begin with light material such as stories from Thurber, or familiar Biblical passages.

Arch of Triumph

To his great satisfaction, he found the servicemen extremely responsive. Alone in a hospital ward or a small auditorium, without the technical equipment of his craft, Laughton found himself warmly and enthusiastically accepted as an individual embodiment of theatre.

Not long after Carole Lombard's death in a plane crash while on a tour selling War Bonds, Laughton went on such a tour himself. After sixteen days on

the road, with only three hours' sleep, he began a marathon campaign at eight one morning over New York's radio station WEAF. He continued talking, reading, acting, exhorting, answering phones and taking pledges, declaiming the Gettysburg Address and snatches from his other great portrayals, for seventeen uninterrupted hours. Telethons on behalf of charity are commonplace now, but his feat was unprecedented then. When he was done, he had

sold more than $300,000 worth of bonds, and his great voice was, for the moment, totally gone.

Through the middle forties, the parade of turkeys with Laughton in undemanding roles continued: *The Suspect,* a murder mystery with Ella Raines, directed by Robert Siodmak; *Captain Kidd,* in which he blustered his way through a weak script attempting to wring some life out of a hopeless situation; *Because of Him,* in which he rejoined Deanna Durbin to play

a ham actor.

Laughton took these parts and the large fees he still commanded for them, and continued his attempt to create for himself another identity with more substance than Hollywood seemed willing to grant him.

His flight beyond acting led him to become interested in working with and coaching acting students, and he devoted considerable time to a group which was preparing works of Shakespeare, Chekhov and

other classics. Among them was Shelley Winters, soon to launch her own career.

Some of the young actors became interested in the work of Bertolt Brecht, and began an experimental production of his *Galileo*. Laughton quickly sensed the dramatic possibilities and was soon supervising the translation and adaptation of the script, casting, sets, and the entire project, as well as playing the leading role.

Well received in Hollywood, the production was brought to New York for a Broadway run. Amid growing criticism of the play, not so much on artistic grounds as because of the author's Communism, Laughton let himself be persuaded by his friends to withdraw from the production. Laughton's interest in the play had undoubtedly been far more theatrical than political, with perhaps some sympathy for the plight of Galileo beset by the forces of ignorance;

The Man on the Eiffel Tower

it was widely felt that he had naively let himself be used in a propaganda effort.

In Hollywood again, Laughton was cast as a sadistic judge in *The Paradine Case*, directed by Alfred Hitchcock. This time, apparently, there was less friction and disagreement between the two, and Laughton displayed some of his old elegance.

His next appearance was a guest role as a minister who reads a Bible passage — capitalizing on his

lecture-circuit specialty in those years — in a film released as *A Miracle Can Happen,* later known as *On Our Merry Way.* The picture featured Burgess Meredith, Paulette Goddard, Fred MacMurray, Hugh Herbert, Jimmy Stewart, Dorothy Lamour, Victor Moore, Henry Fonda, William Demarest, and an assortment of other specialty actors, each doing his thing.

Laughton was a villain again in *The Big Clock,* a better-than-ordinary mystery in which Laughton, as an evil publisher, tries to implicate Ray Milland in his mistress's murder and meets his end by falling down an elevator shaft.

He then played a Nazi villain, quite badly, in an expensive dud for Ingrid Bergman and Charles Boyer, *Arch of Triumph.* In *Girl from Manhattan,* a Dorothy Lamour picture, he played a bishop. In *The Bribe,* starring Robert Taylor and Ava Gardner,

The Blue Veil

Laughton was back in the tropics, wearing his rumpled seersucker and exuding sweat and penny-ante mischief from every pore.

The Man on the Eiffel Tower was a more interesting project. Burgess Meredith and Franchot Tone had acquired the film rights to a Georges Simenon novel and were going to produce it themselves, filming in Paris. Laughton was invited to join them, playing Inspector Maigret and relieving Meredith as di-

rector when the latter had a scene to play. The resulting film was intelligent and well-made, but did not enjoy more than passing success.

Still, it was the first film featuring Laughton in color, and it must have been a refreshing interlude for him in a career that was, after such a happy start, in serious decline.

The Strange Door

Laughton Finds Laughton

More and more in the 1940s, Laughton poured his energies into his readings.

What began as appearances in service hospitals had grown into national tours for which he was now almost better known, especially to young audiences, than for his films.

He had, with his painstaking method, worked out his stage appearances to perfection.

Typically, his entrance from the wings of some

O'Henry's Full House

drafty hall or high school auditorium in the provinces would be to waddle out, heavily scarfed, bent backward to counter the weight of a tall stack of books cradled in his arms.

As the welcoming applause and chuckles continued, he would carefully deposit and arrange the books on tables set out near his lectern, then pull out still more tiny volumes from his pockets as he began his introductory remarks.

The audience would eventually subside into silence, comfortably assured of an engrossing and pleasant evening. The harmless man before them was clearly purged of his former evil ways at last.

And then from Laughton would burst forth a beautiful torrent. The Thurber, a Shakespeare sonnet, a fragment of some brilliant role, the Scripture, and some rolling and endless passage from Thomas Wolfe, replete with the hooting night trains, the

128

heady scents, the dark pre-occupations of the brooding and smoldering South, as recalled by a raving and ruminating exile son condemned for life to catalog his poignant recollection of its myriad aspects.

It was great theatre.

In these solo appearances Laughton developed a new communication with the public, on a more informal and flexible level. By his choice of material, he could accommodate himself to the immediacy of

the situation and mood, and manipulate the contact as he had never been able to within the confines of a single character.

In one sense he was discovering how to move beyond acting; yet in another sense it was still the projection of a single character, after all — the character whose many facets he had employed piecemeal through the years to create his most telling effects. The character was Charles Laughton.

In 1950, Laughton and his producer, Paul Gregory, formed a company that was an outgrowth of the readings: the Drama Quartet, consisting of Sir Cedric Hardwicke, Agnes Moorehead, Charles Boyer, and Laughton himself. Their vehicle was the unperformed third act of Shaw's *Man and Superman,* titled *Don Juan in Hell.*

The conception was an analogy to chamber music; the performers appeared in evening dress, seated

on stools before music stands holding their scripts. There was no scenery, no props. The simplicity of this arrangement made it possible for them to appear anywhere they chose throughout the country — in schools, churches, and even gymnasiums.

Despite the intellectual nature of the work, the utter lack of action, and the austerity of the spectacle, the vocal power and superb talent of the cast made the tour an overwhelming success, and the

group decided to risk a short run on Broadway. It stayed there the better part of a year.

During the run, Laughton busied himself with a stage adaptation of Stephen Vincent Benet's *John Brown's Body,* and recruited a trio composed of Tyrone Power, Judith Anderson, and Raymond Massey to perform it in similar concert readings, directing the production himself. It toured with like success.

Meanwhile, Laughton and his group took *Don Juan* to London during the Festival of Britain.

On his return, Laughton went to Hollywood to appear in *The Blue Veil,* a script by the outstanding writer of the radio era, Norman Corwin, whose films never achieved the same persuasive magic. Laughton played a warm and kindly widower who proposes to Jane Wyman, is turned down, and settles for his secretary instead.

His next appearance was in Universal's *The*

**Abbott and Costello
Meet Captain Kidd**

132

Strange Door, based on a Robert Louis Stevenson tale. In it, Laughton played an evil nobleman who has kept his brother locked in the cellar for twenty years, and is punished by drowning horribly. His brother was played by Karloff, who had surrendered to type-casting almost at once, and been through strange doors, indeed, in the intervening years.

It was not until 1952 that Laughton was once again given the chance to create a deft characteri-

zation, although a brief one, as the repentant bum ironically arrested in *The Cop and the Anthem*, an episode in *O'Henry's Full House*. In one scene with Laughton, Marilyn Monroe had a one-line part.

In the 1950s Laughton also played King Herod in Rita Hayworth's *Salome*, parodied his hamming pirate in *Abbott and Costello Meet Captain Kidd*, and offered a weak-tea echo of his great Henry VIII in Jean Simmons' *Young Bess*.

In 1953, Laughton's producer announced plans for Laughton to return to the stage in *Lord Pengo*, an adaptation by S. N. Behrman of his New Yorker sketches of the art dealer, Joseph Duveen.

Instead, Laughton's next Broadway venture was as co-producer with Paul Gregory of a dramatization of the court martial scene in the Herman Wouk novel *The Caine Mutiny*. Laughton directed Henry Fonda as Lieutenant Greenwald, who defends a

Salome

group of young officers who save their ship from the unbalanced Captain Queeg, played by Lloyd Nolan. The play and Laughton's direction were widely praised.

In Alexander Korda's film *Hobson's Choice,* based on a favorite English sentimental play, Laughton had his biggest screen role in ten years, with David Lean directing.

Returning to Hollywood, Laughton directed a com-

plete film for the first time: *Night of the Hunter,* with Robert Mitchum as a psychopathic preacher after Lillian Gish's hidden treasure. It was properly eerie and haunting.

Back on Broadway, Laughton directed Glynis Johns, Burgess Meredith, Eli Wallach and Cornelia Otis Skinner in Shaw's *Major Barbara,* playing Andrew Undershaft himself.

In 1957, Billy Wilder offered him the part of the lawyer in *Witness for the Prosecution,* and Laughton fell upon it with zest. Elsa Lanchester plays the nurse who attempts to restrain him from overexciting himself as he unravels the truth in the case. It was Laughton's most enjoyable and skillful movie performance in years, and won him, for the third time, an Academy Award nomination as Best Actor. Unfortunately for Laughton, it was the year Alec Guinness built *The Bridge on the River Kwai.*

In 1959 Laughton fulfilled a long-standing desire to play King Lear, with the company at Stratford-on-Avon. Shakespeare was still a formidable opponent, but the notice in the London Times called it "a superb essay in stage pathos."

While still abroad, he played a small role as a British admiral in *Under Ten Flags*, a World War II melodrama, then returned to Hollywood to play a Roman senator in Stanley Kubrick's *Spartacus*, for

which minor part he received star billing.

For a time, he confined his activities to a few television parts and helping Elsa prepare a one-woman show which she toured in the early 1960s.

Otto Preminger, filming a major production in 1962 of Allen Drury's best-seller about Washington, *Advise and Consent*, called upon Laughton to play Seab Cooley, the Southern senator who wields enormous power over national affairs. What Preminger expected was a vicious lampoon of the type; what Laughton gave him was a carefully reasoned, fully credible creation with all the evil present, but wrapped in a kind of sweltering, white-suited dignity. It was a thoroughly professional, well-polished job, and it was Laughton's last.

Even before the film was released it became known that Laughton had cancer. He nevertheless planned to play a bistro proprietor in *Irma la Douce*,

and had begun growing a mustache for the part. Still wearing it, he was taken to the hospital in September of 1962.

On December 15 of that year, Charles Laughton was beyond acting at last.

140

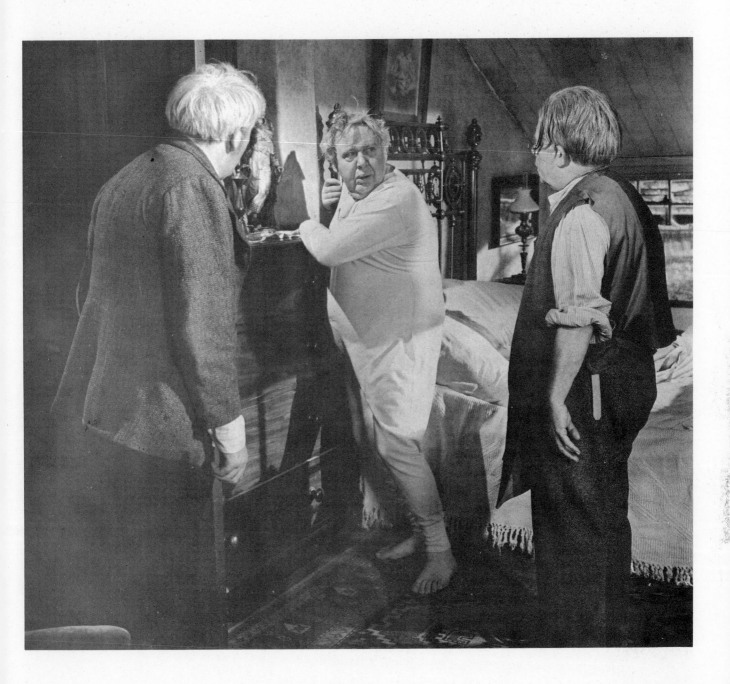

Laughton

If the start of Laughton's unusual career had been deferred because of his personal circumstances, it had blazed quickly into brilliance, as if to make up for the delay.

In his first three years on the professional stage, he had played a dazzling succession of varied parts and become a noted star while still in his twenties.

In seven more years, he had appeared in sixteen films, some negligible, some among the best the

142

screen has produced to this day, and had earned a place among the film immortals, still in his middle thirties.

Then, overnight, his pre-eminence crumbled almost to obscurity, he spent his forties virtually in limbo.

It was not the familiar problem of the matinee idol disintegrating with the passing years; Laughton had never made his reputation as a romantic lead,

Witness for the Prosecution

but as a dominant figure with a certain malevolent touch. There had been no diminution of his talent, as occasional flashes of brilliance showed even in his worst films. What went wrong?

Those who revelled with him in his best work and agonized with him through the fallow years may point with outrage to the film industry on both sides of the Atlantic for their often pedestrian use of a magnificent dramatic potential.

Those who saw him only as a glandular case exposed to vocational training may counter that his was the sin of sloth, that the accident of early fame was compounded by his lack of taste in the parts he accepted to produce an over-rated commodity which could be had for any purpose for a price.

Certainly it is true that he aquiesced in the debasement of his ability to project subtle wickedness; that when perverted to the gross uses of horror it

Under Ten Flags

became simply grotesque. In those troubled years, the excesses of monsters who were all too real came to pre-empt the field of terror and make even the Gothic creations of Karloff and Lugosi seem almost congenial — and finally comic. The fine malice of a Laughton called for scripts that were not to be found.

And it must finally be said that his bulk acted as a limitation on his range, versatile as he was.

Spartacus

Overweight, of course, is more than an actor's problem; it is a fact which confronts large men from the time they are the butt of heartless school friends, through their young manhood when they are unacceptable to the great majority of possible mates, to their mature years when they find themselves at the center of great events only if they have found some transcendant virtue — or unwholesome force — that places them there despite it.

Flesh can become an imprisoning cell, inducing an inaccessible privacy of spirit. The distance beyond to villain and monster is short; self-satisfaction and supercilious pride are steps along the way. It is no wonder we saw him so often set adrift, drowned, set upon by beasts, hurtling into pits. The arrogant bastard had it coming, we were privileged and delighted to feel. At the best of his worst, he had a hot line to our gut chemicals processes of hate for

Advise and Consent

the fat boy.

It was, in a way, his priceless curse. You couldn't learn it at the Royal Academy, or pick it up on weekends in the country, or get it by osmosis walking through a palace. You had it or you didn't, and if you did it would pay your bills if you let it. For a time, perhaps he did. If so, he paid his dues for that.

It was not until his readings that he broke out of prison and began to try and get on with it in spite

of going up and coming down and losing it all somewhere in the middle.

Laughton was in Wilmington on his reading tour the same day the *Caine Mutiny* company came to town, so he went with a friend and stood in the back of the theatre and watched the matinee.

The play reached the scene at the end when the court martial is over and the lawyer, Barney Greenwald, having just destroyed Captain Queeg, joins the young officers he has cleared for a drink, then stays on to get smashed and lay them out for ruining a man who tried to do his job and win the war and keep Hitler from turning people into soap and ashes.

Laughton had helped to build that scene, had told Fonda just how he thought it should be played, but now he stands with tears streaming down his face, whispering hoarsely to his friend, "*I can't help it!*

I can't help it! It always makes me cry!''

Why is Charles Laughton crying?

Is it the script? The performance? Free-floating sentimentality, waiting to be triggered off?

Is he off in his boat on a Pacific of injustice that stretches all the way to Scarborough and the front desk and too many dreams deferred, through the painstaking acquisition of externals and credentials that lead only to betrayal, centuries ago, off the

M.S.-27

island of lost souls, when he himself tried to put down a rebellious crew and failed?

Recognition for an actor may come in many forms.

CHARLES LAUGHTON'S MOVIE CREDITS:

Piccadilly (1929)

BIP. Directed by E. A. Dupont. Cast: Gilda Gray, Jameson Thomas, Anna May Wong, King Ho-Chang, Cyril Ritchard, Hannah Jones. Laughton had a bit part as an ill-mannered diner who interrupted Gilda Gray's dance number. A silent, save for music.

Wolves (1930)

British and Dominion Productions. Directed by Albert De Courville. Cast: Dorothy Gish, Malcolm Keen, Jack Ostermann, Arthur Margetson, Franklyn Bellamy, Griffith Humphreys, Andrews Engelmann, Betty Bolton. Laughton, as a renegade, lost his life helping Miss Gish escape from a whaling camp. A horribly mangled version was released in the US as *Wanted Men*.

Down River (1931)

Gaumont. Directed by Peter Godfrey. Cast: Harold Huth, Jane Baxter. A routine programmer.

The Old Dark House (1932)

Universal. Directed by James Whale. Cast: Boris Karloff, Melvyn Douglas, Gloria Stuart, Lillian Bond, Ernest Thesiger, Eva Moore, Raymond Massey, Brember Wills, John Dudgeon. Laughton's first US film was an eerie tale of people isolated in Wales during a bad storm. Laughton had a small role as a Lancashire knight.

The Devil and the Deep (1932)

Paramount. Directed by Marion Gering. Cast: Gary Cooper, Tallulah Bankhead, Cary Grant, Paul Porcasi, Juliette Compton, Henry Kolker, Dorothy Christy, Arthur Hoyt. Jealous submarine-captain Laughton attempts to drown his wife (Bankhead) and mate (Cooper), but meets a watery end himself.

Payment Deferred (1932)

Metro Goldwyn Mayer. Directed by Lothar Mendes. Cast: Neil Hamilton, Maureen O'Sullivan, Dorothy Peterson, Verree Teasdale, Ray Milland, Billy Bevan, William Stack, Halliwell Hobbes. Repeating his stage role, Laughton played the pathetic murderer who inadvertently drives his wife to suicide.

The Sign of the Cross (1932)

Paramount. Directed by Cecil B. DeMille. Cast: Frederic March, Elissa Landi, Claudette Colbert, Ian Keith, Harry Beresford, Arthur Hohl, Tommy Conlon, Clarence Burton, Harold Healy, Robert Manning, Vivian Tobin, Ferdinand Gottschalk, Joyzelle Joyner, Nat Pendleton, William V. Mong, Richard Alexander, Jo Bonomo. Laughton played Nero as an effeminate fop.

If I Had a Million (1932)

Paramount. Directed by Ernst Lubitsch, Norman Taurog, Stephen Roberts. Norman McLeon, James Cruze, William A. Seiter, H. Bruce Humberstone. Cast: Gary Cooper, George Raft, Wynne Gibson, Jack Oakie, Frances Dee, Charles Ruggles, Alison Skipworth, W. C. Fields, Mary Boland, Roscoe Karns, May Robson, Gene Raymond, Lucien Littlefield, and Richard Bennett as the millionaire. In the Lubitsch-directed episode lowly clerk Laughton razzed his boss and left his job.

Island of Lost Souls (1933)

Paramount. Directed by Erle Kenton. Cast: Bela Lugosi, Richard Arlen, Leila Hyams, Kathleen Burke, Arthur Hohl, Stanley Fields, Robert Kortman, Tetsu Komai, Hans Steinke, Harry Ekezian, Rosemary Grimes, Paul Hurst, George Irving. Laughton was a mad scientist killed by the monsters he created.

Private Life of Henry VIII (1933)

London Films. Directed by Alexander Korda. Cast: Robert Donat, Lady Tree, Binnie Barnes, Elsa Lanchester, Merle Oberon, Franklyn Dyall, Miles Mander, Wendy Barrie, Claude Allister, John Loder, Everely Gregg, Lawrence Hanray, William Austin, John Turnbull, Frederick Cully, Gibb McLaughlin, Sam Livesey. Laughton won his only Oscar for playing Henry as a man who wanted to be loved not for his crown but for himself. The first foreign-made film to win an Academy Award.

White Woman (1933)

Paramount. Directed by Stuart Walker. Cast: Carole Lombard, Charles Bickford, Kent Taylor, Percy Kilbride, Charles B. Middleton, James Bell, Claude King, Ethel Griffies. Tepid melodrama with Laughton losing his jungle empire in a native revolt, and hs wife (Lombard) to Taylor.

The Barretts of Wimpole Street (1934)

Metro Goldwyn Mayer. Directed by Sidney Franklin. Cast: Norma Shearer, Fredric March, Maureen O'Sullivan, Katherine Alexander, Una O'Connor, Ian Wolfe, Marion Clayton, Ralph Forbes, Vernon Downing, Neville Clark, Matthew Smith, Robert Carleton, Allan Conrad, Peter Hobbes, Ferdinand Munier, Leo G. Carroll. Laughton was Mr. Barrett. On tv this film is now called *Forbidden Alliance*.

Ruggles of Red Gap (1935)

Paramount. Directed by Leo McCarey. Cast: Mary Boland, Zasu Pitts, Roland Young, Leila Hyams. In one of his best-remembered comedy roles, Laughton was an English butler in the American West.

Les Miserables (1935)

United Artists. Directed by Richard Boleslawsky. Cast: Fredric March, Cedric Hardwicke, Rochelle Hudson, Florence Eldridge, Jessie Ralph, Frances Drake, John Beal. Laughton was Javert.

Mutiny on the Bounty (1935)

Metro Goldwyn Mayer. Directed by Frank Lloyd. Cast: Clark Gable, Franchot Tone, Dudley Digges, Herbert Mundin, Eddie Quillan, Donald Crisp, Henry Stephenson, Spring Byington, Movita. His Captain Bligh is perhaps Laughton's best remembered portrayal.

Rembrandt (1936)

London Films. Directed by Alexander Korda. Cast: Gertrude Lawrence, Elsa Lanchester, Edward Chapman, John Clements, Marius Goring, Raymond Huntley, Herbert Lomas, John Bryning, Walter Hudd. Laughton portrayed Rembrandt from the height of his fame to his poverty-stricken old age.

I, Claudius (1936)

London Films: Directed by Josef von Sternberg. Cast: Merle Oberon, Flora Robson, Robert Newton, Emlyn Williams. In this ill-fated production, Laughton was cast as Tiberius Claudius Drusus, the stuttering cripple who became an emperor. It was never finished.

Vessel of Wrath (1938)

(In the US: *The Beachcomber*). Mayflower-Paramount. Directed by Erich Pommer. Cast: Elsa Lanchester, Tyrone Guthrie, Robert Newton, Dolly Mollinger, Rosita Garcia, J. Solomon, Fred Groves, Eliot Makeham, Mahfoo Ley On, D. J. Ward, S. Alley and "Dudley" (the terrier). Laughton, as a bum with no scruples, combatted aggressive spinster Lanchester.

St. Martin's Lane (1939)

(In the US: *Sidewalks of London*). Mayflower-Paramount. Directed by Tim Whelan. Cast: Vivian Leigh, Rex Harrison, Larry Adler, Tyrone Guthrie, Gus McNaughton, Bart Cormack, Edward Lexy, Marie O'Neill, Basil Gill, Claire Greet, David Burns, Cyril Smith, Helen Haye, Ronald Ward. London street-singer Laughton helps Leigh become a musical star.

Jamaica Inn (1939)

Associated British-Paramount. Directed by Alfred Hitchcock. Cast: Maureen O'Hara, Leslie Banks, Emlyn Williams, Robert Newton, Marie Ney, Wylie Watson, Morland Graham, Edwin Greenwood, Mervyn Johns, Stephen Haggard, Horace Hodges, Hay Petrie, Frederick Piper, Herbert Lomas, Claire Greet, Jeanne de Casalis, Bromley Davenport, Mabel Terry Lewis, George Curzon, Basil Radford. Laughton was the secret leader of a murderous band of shipwreckers.

The Hunchback of Notre Dame (1939)

RKO. Directed by William Dieterle. Cast: Cedric Hardwick, Thomas Mitchell, Maureen O'Hara, Edmond O'Brien, Alan Marshal, Walter Hampden, Katherine Alexander, Harry Davenport, George Zucco, Fritz Leiber, Etienne Girardot, Helen Whitney, Minna Gombell, Arthur Hohl, George Tobias, Rod La Rocque, Spencer Charters. As Quasimodo, Laughton was unrecognizable.

They Knew What They Wanted (1940)

RKO. Directed by Garson Kanin. Cast: Carole Lombard, William Gargan, Harry Carey, Frank Fay, Joe Bernard, Janet Fox, Lee Tung-Foo, Karl Malden, Victor Kilian, Paul Lepere. Laughton was the uneducated Italian-American and Lombard his mail-order bride.

It Started With Eve (1941)

Universal. Directed by Henry Koster. Cast: Deanna Durbin, Robert Cummings, Guy Kibbee, Margaret Tallichet, Catherine Doucet, Walter Catlert, Charles Coleman, Leonard Elliott, Irving Bacon, Gus Schilling, Wade Boteler, Dorothea Kent, Clara Blandick. He was the elderly matchmaker.

The Tuttles of Tahiti (1942)

RKO. Directed by Charles Vidor. Cast: Jon Hall, Peggy Drake, Victor Francen, Gene Reynolds, Florence Bates, Curt Bois, Adeline de Walt Reynolds, Mala, Leonard Sues, Jody Gilbert, Tommy Cook, Jack Carr, Jimmy Ames. Laughton played the head of a wacky family in this South Seas.

Tales of Manhattan (1942)

20th Century-Fox. Directed by Julien Duvivier. In this all-star special Laughton was the penniless musician whose rented tail coat splits apart at the seams when he is suddenly afforded an opportunity to conduct at Carnegie Hall.

Stand By For Action (1942)

Metro Goldwyn Mayer. Directed by Robert Z. Leonard. Robert Taylor, Brian Donlevy, Walter Brennan, Marilyn Maxwell, Henry O'Neill, Marta Linden, Chill Wills, Douglas Dumbrille, Richard Quine, William Tannen, Douglas Fowley, Tim Ryan, Dcik Simmons, Byron Foulger, Hobart Cavanaugh, Inez Cooper, Ben Weldon, Harry Fleischman. Laughton was somewhat mis-cast as a Rear Admiral of World War II.

Forever And A Day (1943)

RKO. Seven directors and producers, 79 stars. In a mid-Victorian comedy segment of this all-starrer Laughton was a butler.

This Land Is Mine (1943)

RKO. Directed by Jean Renoir. Cast: Maureen O'Hara, George Sanders, Walter Slezak, Kent Smith, Una O'Connor, Philip Merivale, Thurston Hall, George Coulouris, Nancy Gates, Ivan Simpson, John Donat, Frank Alton, Leo Bulgakov, Wheaton Chambers, Cecil Weston. As a cowardly French schoolteacher during the Nazi occupation, he is forced to defend himself against a false murder charge and becomes brave in the face of death.

The Man From Down Under (1943)

Metro Goldwyn Mayer. Directed by Robert Z. Leonard. Cast: Binnie Barnes, Richard Carlson, Donna Reed, Christopher Severn, Clyde Cook, Horace McNally, Arthur Shields, Evelyn Falke, Hobart Cavanaugh, Andre Charlot. Australian bar-owner Laughton courted and battled Binnie Barnes, match-made Carlson and Donna Reed, coped with World War II.

The Canterville Ghost (1944)

Metro Goldwyn Mayer. Directed by Jules Dassin. Cast: Robert Young, Margaret O'Brien, William Gargan, Reginald Owen, Rags Ragland, Una O'Connor, Donald Stuart, Peter Lawford, Elizabeth Risdon, Frank Faylen, Lumsden Hare, William Moss, Bobby Readick, Marc Cramer. Laughton was a 17th Century ghost.

The Suspect (1944)

Universal. Directed by Robert Siodmak. Cast: Ella Raines, Dean Harens, Stanley Ridges, Henry Danieli, Rosalind Ivan, Molly Lamont, Raymond Severn, Eve Amber, Maude Eburne, Clifford Brooke. Laughton murders his nagging wife and unsuccessfully attempts to start a new life with Miss Raines.

Captain Kidd (1945)

United Artists. Directed by Rowland V. Lee. Cast: Randolph Scott, Barbara Britton, Reginald Owen, John Carradine, Gilbert Roland, John Qualen, Sheldon Leonard, Abner Biberman, Henry Daniel, William Farnum, Miles Mander, Ray Teale. He had the title role.

Because of Him (1946)

Universal. Directed by Richard Wallace. Cast: Deanna Durbin, Franchot Tone, Helen Broderick, Stanley Ridges, Donald Meek, Charles Halton, Regina Wallace, Douglas Wood, Lynn Whitney. As a famous ham actor he gets involved with aspiring actress Durbin and playwright Tone.

The Paradine Case (1948)

Selznick. Directed by Alfred Hitchcock. Cast: Gregory Peck, Ann Todd, Charles Coburn, Ethel Barrymore, Valli, Louis Jourdan, Joan Tetzel, Leo G. Carroll. Laughton was the sadistic judge.

The Big Clock (1948)

Paramount. Directed by John Farrow. Cast: Ray Milland, Maureen O'Sullivan, George Macready, Rita Johnson, Elsa Lanchester, Harold Vermilyea, Dan Tobin, Henry ("Harry") Morgan, Richard Webb. Publishing tycoon Laughton tries to pin the murder of his mistress on innocent editor Milland, and falls down an empty elevator shaft.

Arch of Triumph (1948)

Enterprise-United Artists. Directed by Lewis Milestone. Cast: Ingrid Bergman, Charles Boyer, Louis Calhern, Roman Bohnen, Stephen Berkassy, Ruth Nelson, Curt Bois, J. Edward Bromberg, Michael Romanoff, Art Smith, John Laurenz, Leon Lenoir, Franco Corsaro, Nino Pipitoni, Vladimir Rashevsky, Alvin Hammer, Jay Gilpin, Ilia Kharma, Andre Marsauden, Hazel Brooks, Byron Foulger, Bill Conrad, Peter Virgo, Fedor Chaliapin. Nazi agent Laughton hunts refugee Boyer and is eventually killed by him.

The Girl from Manhattan (1948)

United Artists. Directed by Alfred E. Green. Cast: Dorothy Lamour, George Montgomery, Ernest Truex, Hugh Herbert, Constance Collier, William Frawley, Sara Allgood, Frank Orth, Howard Freeman, Raymond Largay, George Chandler, Selmer Jackson, Adeline De Walt Reynolds, Maurice Cass, Eddy Waller. In this Dorothy Lamour programmer he was a bishop.

The Bribe (1949)

Metro Goldwyn Mayer. Directed by Robert Z. Leonard. Cast: Robert Taylor, Ava Gardner, John Hodiak, Vincent Price. Laughton hammed it up in a small role as a treacherous stumble-bum in a tropical hotel.

The Man on the Eiffel Tower (1949)

RKO. Directed by Budgess Meredith. Cast: Franchot Tone, Burgess Meredith, Robert Hutton, Jean Wallace, Patricia Roc, Belita, George Thorpe, William Phipps, William Cottrell, Chaz Chase, Wilfrid Hyde-White. As Inspector Maigret he patiently tracks down murderer Tone. Laughton's first color film.

The Blue Veil (1951)

RKO. Directed by Curtis Bernhardt. Cast: Jane Wyman, Joan Blondell, Richard Carlson, Agnes Moorehead, Don Taylor, Audrey Totter, Cyril Cusack, Everett Sloane, Natalie Wood, Warner Anderson, Alan Napier, Henry ("Harry") Morgan, Vivian Vance, Les Tremayne, John Ridgely, Dan O'Herlihy, Carleton G. Young, Dan Seymour. In the inital episode Laughton is a kindly widower who proposes marriage unsuccessfully to nurse Wyman and marries his secretary (Vance).

The Strange Door (1951)

Universal-International. Directed by Joseph Pevney. Cast: Boris Karloff, Sally Forrest, Richard Stapley, Michael Pate, Alan Napier, William Cottrell, Morgan Farley, Edwin Parker, Charles Horvath, Paul Cavanaugh. Sadistic nobleman Laughton keeps his brother (Karloff) confined for twenty years and meets a watery death.

O. Henry's Full House (1952)

20th Century Fox. Directed by Henry Koster. In "the Cap and the Anthem" segment, Laughton was a Bowery bum who undergoes a change of heart in church. Marilyn Monroe had a 1-line part.

Abbott and Costello Meet Captain Kidd (1952)

Warner. Directed by Charles Lamont. Cast: Bud Abbott, Lou Costello, Hillary Brooke, Fran Warren, Bill Shirley, Leif Erickson. Laughton re-created his 1945 role in this spoof and romped around in a union-suit.

Salome (1953)

Columbia. Directed by William Dieterle. Cast: Rita Hayworth, Stewart Granger, Judith Anderson, Cedric Hardwck, Alan Badel, Basil Sidney, Maurice Schwartz, Rex Reason, Arnold Moss, Suata & Asoka, Robert Warwick, Carmen D'Antonio, Michael Granger, Karl Davis. He played a leering King Herod.

Young Bess (1953)

Metro Goldwyn Mayer. Directed by George Sidney. Cast: Jean Simmons, Stewart Granger, Deborah Kerr, Kay Walsh, Guy Rolfe, Kathleen Byron, Cecil Kellaway, Rex Thompson, Robert Arthur, Leo G. Carroll, Norma Varden, Alan Napier, Noreen Corocoran, Dawn Addams, Doris Lloyd, Elaine Stewart. He was Henry VIII again.

Hobson's Choice (1954)

London Films. Directed by David Lean. Cast: John Mills, Brenda de Branzie, Daphne Anderson, Prunella Scales, Richard Wattis, Derek Blomfield, Helen Haye, Joseph Tomelty, Julien Mitchell, Gibb McLaughlin, Philip Stainton, Dorothy Gordon, Madge Brindley, John Laurie, Raymond Huntley, Jack Howarth, Herbert C. Walton. He was a blustering widower with three unmarried daughters.

The Night of the Hunter (1955)

United Artists. Directed by Charles Laughton. Cast: Robert Mitchum, Shelley Winters, Lillian Gish, Evelyn Varden, Peter Graves, Billy Chapin, Sally Jane Bruce, James Gleason, Don Beddoe, Gloria Castillo, Mary Ellen Clemons, Cheryl Gallaway. The only complete film Laughton directed.

Witness for the Prosecution (1957)

United Artists. Directed by Billy Wilder. Cast: Tyrone Power, Marlene Dietrich, Elsa Lanchester, John Williams, Henry Daniell, Ian Wolfe, Una O'Connor, Torin Thatcher, Francis Compton. Laughton was the lawyer who was bossed by his nurse (Lanchester).

Under Ten Flags (1960)

Paramount-DeLaurentiis. Directed by Duilio Coletti. Cast: Van Heflin, Mylene Demongeot, John Ericson, Liam Redmond, Alex Nicol, Cecil Parker, Gregoire Aslan, Eleanora Rossi-Drago, Gianmaria Volonte, Philo Hauser, Dieter Eppler, Ralph Truman, Peter Carsten, Folco Lulli. Laughton had a small role as a British admiral.

Spartacus (1960)

United-International. Directed by Stanley Kubrick. Cast: Kirk Douglas, Laurence Olivier, Jean Simmons, Peter Ustinov, John Gavin, Tony Curtis, Nina Foch, Herbert Lom, John Ireland, John Dall, Charles McGraw, Joanna Barnes, Harold J. Stone, Woody Strode, Peter Brocco, Paul Lambert, Robert J. Wilke, Nicholas Dennis, John Hoyt, Frederick Worlock, Dayton Lummis. Laughton was a Roman Senator.

Advise and Consent (1962)

Columbia. Directed by Otto Preminger. Cast: Franchot Tone, Lew Ayres, Henry Fonda, Walter Pidgeon, Don Murray, Peter Lawford, Gene Tierney, Burgess Meredith, Eddie Hodges, Paul Ford, George Grizzard, Inga Swenson, Paul McGrath, Will Geer, Edward Andrews, Betty White, Malcolm Atterbury, J. Edward McKinley, Tom Helmore, John Granger, Chet Stratton. In his last role he gave a fine performance as a Southern Senator.

ADDENDA

Page 15 — QUO VADIS: The version in which Peter Ustinov portrayed Nero (1951; MGM) was produced by Sam Zimbalist and directed by Mervyn LeRoy.

Page 20 — Charles Laughton was born on July 1, 1899.

Page 39 — The third short film was not ON THE SPOT, but was entitled FRANKIE AND JOHNNY. ON THE SPOT was a stage play by Edgar Wallace, that Laughton did on the London stage in 1930.

Page 47 — Column 2, line 6: J. B. *Priestley*.

Page 51 — Column 1, paragraph 3, line 2: *temperaments*.

Page 54 — The title is ISLAND OF LOST SOULS.

Page 85 — Paragraph 2, line 3: *Sydney*, Australia.

Page 95 — Paragraph 1, line 3: CYRANO is Edmond Rostand's famed play CYRANO DE BERGERAC.

Page 95 — Column 2, line 5: The play Laughton performed in French was Moliere's LE MEDECIN MALGRE LUI (The Doctor in Spite of Himself).

Page 103 — Column 2, line 3: J. B. *Priestley*.

Page 124 — Paragraph 2, line 1: A BATTLE OF NERVES is the title of the Georges Simenon novel.

Page 129 — Column 2, line 3: This group was formally known as The *First* Drama Quartet.

Column 2, line 6: The third act of MAN AND SUPERMAN was not "unperformed," but, rather, never performed with the rest of the play, due to its length. The third act is also known as DON JUAN IN HELL.

Page 135 — Paragraph 1, line 1: *THE* NIGHT OF THE HUNTER.